Imagine²

WORKBOOK

Rachel Wilson

COURSE CONSULTANTS

Elaine Boyd

Paul Dummett

NATIONAL GEOGRAPHIC
LEARNING

Australia • Brazil • Canada • Mexico • Singapore • United Kingdom • United States

National Geographic Learning,
a Cengage Company

Imagine 2 Workbook

Author: Rachel Wilson

Course Consultants: Elaine Boyd, Paul Dummett

Publisher: Rachael Gibbon

Executive Editor: Joanna Freer

Project Manager: Samantha Grey

Editorial Assistant: Polly McLachlan

Director of Global Marketing: Ian Martin

Product Marketing Manager: Fernanda De Oliveira

Heads of Strategic Marketing:

  Charlotte Ellis (Europe, Middle East and Africa)

  Justin Kaley (Asia and Greater China)

  Irina Pereyra (Latin America)

Senior Content Project Manager: Beth McNally

Senior Media Researcher: Leila Hishmeh

Senior Art Director: Brenda Carmichael

Operations Support: Rebecca G. Barbush, Hayley
  Chwazik-Gee

Manufacturing Manager: Eyvett Davis

Composition: Composure

For permission to use material from this text or product,
submit all requests online at **cengage.com/permissions**
Further permissions questions can be emailed to
permissionrequest@cengage.com

ISBN: 978-0-357-91183-9

National Geographic Learning
Cheriton House, North Way,
Andover, Hampshire, SP10 5BE
United Kingdom

Locate your local office at **international.cengage.com/region**

Visit National Geographic Learning online at **ELTNGL.com**
Visit our corporate website at **www.cengage.com**

Printed in the United Kingdom by Ashford Colour Press Ltd.
Print Number: 02   Print Year: 2024

Imagine **2** WORKBOOK

Welcome 4

1 Back to School 6

2 My Things 12

Units 1–2 Let's Talk p. 18, Video p. 19, Review p. 20

3 At Home 22

4 Let's Play! 28

Units 3–4 Game p. 34, Reading Challenge p. 35, Review p. 36

5 At Work 38

6 My Day 44

Units 5–6 Let's Talk p. 50, Video p. 51, Review p. 52

7 Mealtime 54

8 Celebrate! 60

Units 7–8 Game p. 66, Reading Challenge p. 67, Review p. 68

Word List 70

A Match.

fourteen   thirteen   eleven   fifteen   twelve

11   12   13   14   15   16   17   18   19   20

nineteen   eighteen   sixteen   twenty   seventeen

B Colour.

1.

purple

2.
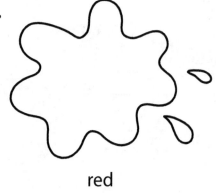
red

3.
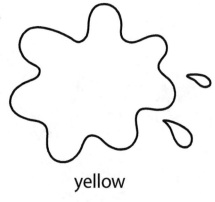
yellow

4.

black

5.

brown

6.
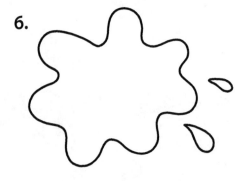
green

C Circle.

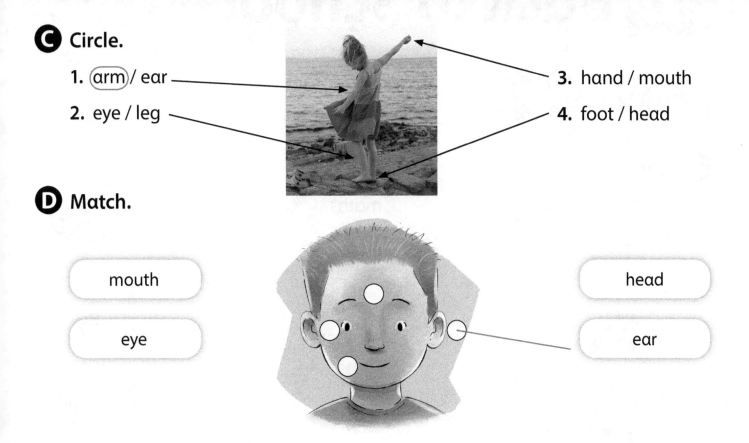

1. (arm)/ ear

2. eye / leg

3. hand / mouth

4. foot / head

D Match.

mouth

eye

head

ear

E Listen, read and circle. 🎧 TR: 0.1

(This is)/ **These are** my mouth.
My mouth is red.
This is / **These are** my ears.
This is / **These are** my head!

This is / **These are** my eyes.
My eyes are blue.
This is / **These are** my hands.
One and two!

1 Back to School

Lesson 1 Vocabulary

A Match.

1.

2.

3.

4.

maths

reading

art

computers

music

PE

science

English

5.

6.
Hello!

7.
3+2=5

8.

B Listen and circle. 🎧 TR: 1.1

1. music   (Yes)/ No   science   Yes / No
2. art   Yes / No   maths   Yes / No
3. PE   Yes / No   reading   Yes / No
4. English   Yes / No   computers   Yes / No

C What do you like? Write in order (☹ to ☺).

 _____ _____ _____ _____

_____ _____ _____ _____

A Listen and write. 🎧 TR: 1.2

Monday, Tuesday – time for school!
Wednesday, Thursday, Friday – time for school!

I've got English on _____ , time for school.
I've got maths _____ Tuesday, time for school.
I've got art _____ , time for school.
_____ music on Thursday, time for school.
_____ . School is cool!

Saturday, Sunday, there's no school!
There's no school. That's cool too!

B Read and tick (✓). Which student has got this timetable?

Monday	Tuesday	Wednesday	Thursday	Friday
reading	PE	English	maths	English
science	maths	reading	science	PE
LUNCH				
maths	English	music	English	reading
art	science	maths	computers	maths

1.
☐
I've got reading on Monday and Thursday.

2.
☐
I've got PE on Tuesday and computers on Wednesday.

3.
☐
I've got art on Monday and music on Wednesday.

A Unscramble the words.

1. t a b o __b__ __o__ __a__ __t__

2. k o r w m o h e __ __ __ __ __ __ __ __

3. i e v r r __ __ __ __ __ __

4. s e l o n s __ __ __ __ __ __ __

B Read and write. 🎧 TR: 1.3

> boat   homework   lessons   river   teacher

Look at this classroom. It's on a _____. This is a boat school in Bangladesh.

It's on a _____. The classroom has got desks and chairs. It hasn't got walls or windows. Students can see plants, trees and the river. It's a very cool school.

In the classroom, there are about thirty students and one _____. The students are boys and girls. Students have got lessons for two or three hours a day, six days a week.

There are _____ in English, maths, science, computers and art. There's _____ too. Have you got homework?

C Read and write a tick (✓) or a cross (✗).

	Boat school	My school
1. There are desks and chairs.	✓	☐
2. There are walls.	☐	☐
3. There are English lessons.	☐	☐
4. There are PE lessons.	☐	☐

A Circle.

1. Have (you) / **she** / **he** got English on Monday?

   Yes, **I** / **she** / **he** have.

2. Has **I** / **you** / **he** got PE on Thursday?

   No, **I** / **you** / **he** hasn't.

B Listen and write *Sofia* or *Marissa*. 🎧 TR: 1.4

1. _____   2. _____

C Look and write.

1. Has Marissa got her homework book?   _____.

2. Has Sofia got her PE shoes?   _____.

3. Has Marissa got a banana?   _____.

4. Has Marissa got a pencil case?   _____.

5. Has Sofia got an apple?   _____.

6. Has Sofia got her school hat?   _____.

A Listen and number. 🎧 TR: 1.5

tank ☐   maths ☐   bat ☐

thank 1   mat ☐   bath ☐

B Help the monkey find the bananas. Find the words with *th*. Then say.

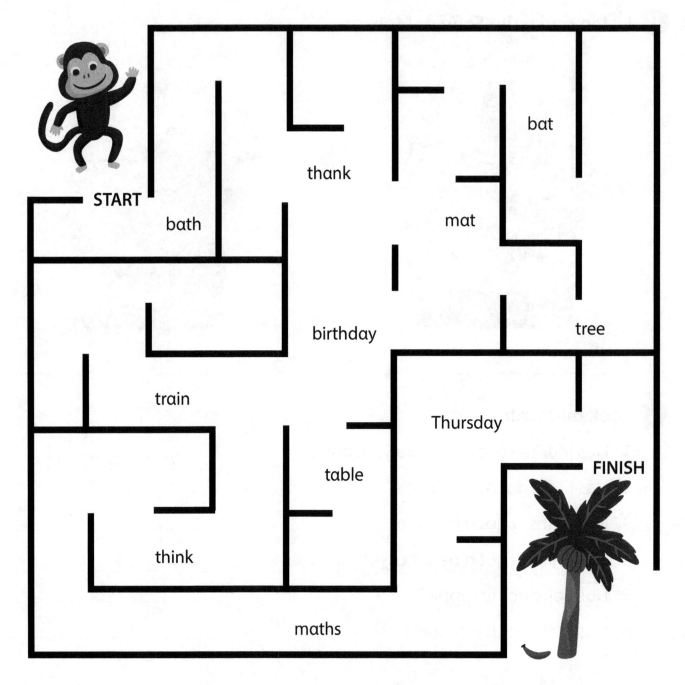

VALUE

Be responsible.

A Look and tick (✓).

1.

B Read. Number the actions in order.
After school ...

1. I play with my toys. `2`

   I do my science homework. `1`

2. I give my cat her dinner. ☐

   I play football. ☐

3. I watch TV. ☐

   I help my mum and dad at home. ☐

C Draw a picture of you being responsible at school or at home.

2 My Things

A Listen and number. Then colour. ∩TR: 2.1

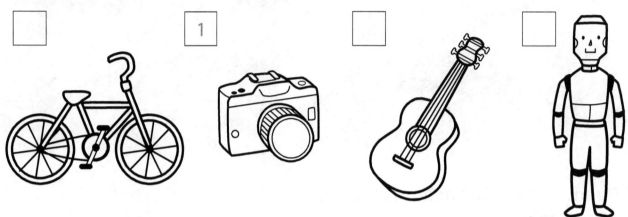

☐   1   ☐   ☐

B Match and write.

1. It's a _____robot_____.

2. It's a _____.

3. They're _____.

4. It's a _____.

5. It's a _____.

6. They're _____.

7. It's a _____.

8. It's a _____.

a.
b.
c.
d.
e.
f.
g.
h.

C Which of these things have you got? Write.

I've got _____.

A **Listen and write.** 🎧 TR: 2.2

Is _____ your skateboard? Can I have a go?

Yes, _____ my skateboard. You can have a go!

Are _____ your building bricks? Can I have a go?

Yes, _____ my building bricks. You can have a go!

B **Look, read and tick (✓).**

1.

| This is my skateboard. ✓ | That's my skateboard. ☐ |

2.

| This isn't my bike. ☐ | That isn't my bike. ☐ |

3.

| These are my felt-tip pens. ☐ | These are my felt-tip pens. ☐ |

4.

| These aren't my pencils. ☐ | Those aren't my pencils. ☐ |

A Circle the words that are opposites.

cool   new   old   walk

B Listen and write. 🎧 TR: 2.3

cool   new   old   robots   short

Claudia Chan Shaw is a toy collector in Australia. She's got lots of _____ toys.
Claudia has got _____ and _____ toys. She really likes toy _____. Look at these robots from her collection!

Claudia has got a robot named Robby. Robby is black. His head is big. His arms and feet are red. He can walk!

Claudia has got another robot called Zoomer. He's more than 60 years old! He's got _____ arms and legs. He can walk too.

C Read and write a tick (✓) or a cross (✗).

1. Robby has got red feet.   ✓

2. Robby has got a small head.   ✗

3. Robby has got a green body.   ☐

4. Robby has got blue arms.   ☐

5. Robby can walk.   ☐

6. Robby can run.   ☐

A **Read and circle.**

1. This is **Sams** / **Sam's** bike.

2. These aren't **Tilly's** / **Tilly** marbles.

3. That's **Zane's** / **Zanes** camera.

4. Those are **Jodys** / **Jody's** building bricks.

B **Listen, look and write.** Does it belong to Jakob or Zara? TR: 2.4

1.

   This is ___Jakob's___ guitar.

3.

   This is _____ camera.

2.

   This is _____ guitar.

4.

   This is _____ camera.

C **Look and write.**

1. The ball is _____Yui's_____.

2. The skateboard is _____.

3. The bike _____.

4. The bag _____.

5. The hat _____.

A Listen and circle the words with *th* as in *this.* 🎧 TR: 2.5

(this)   bath   that   these   maths   those

thank   brother   Thursday   mother   three   think

B Find the words with *th* as in *this.* Colour them red. Then say. What's the hidden picture?

The hidden picture is _____ .

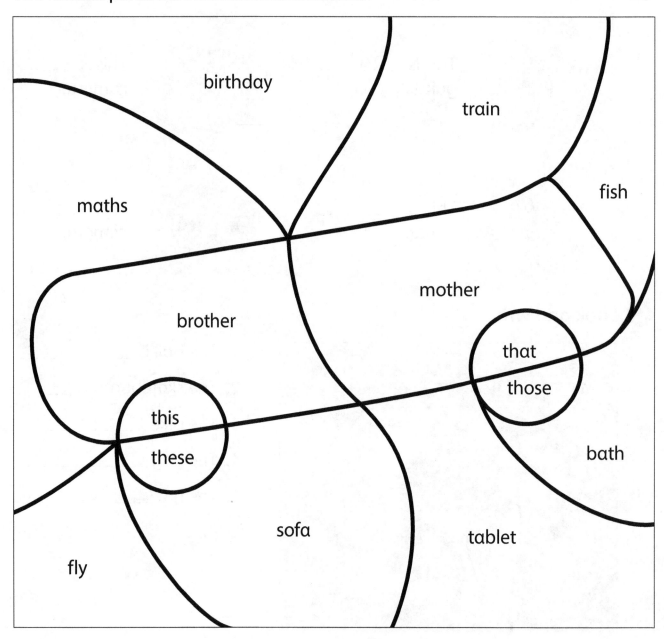

A Look and tick (✓).

B Draw lines to tidy up the bedroom.

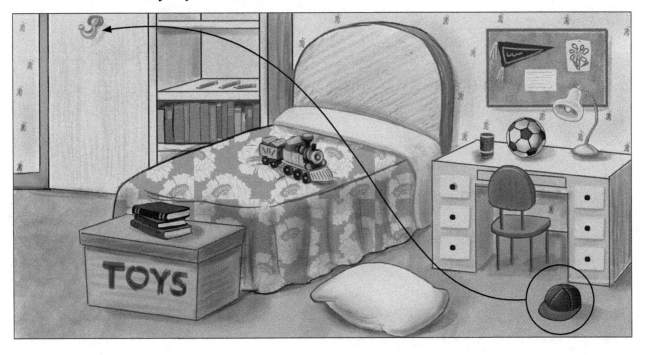

A **Read and circle.** Then listen and check. 🎧 TR: 2.6

Enrico:	Hi, Lee. How are (you) / **they** today?
Lee:	I haven't got a drink, so I'm **thirsty** / **hungry**.
Enrico:	Oh, no! Here, have some water.
Lee:	Thanks. And you? **How** / **Where** are you?
Enrico:	Not good. I'm **angry** / **tired**.
Lee:	Oh, no! What's the **matter** / **homework**?
Enrico:	I can't find my pencil.
Lee:	Here. You can borrow my pencil.
Enrico:	Great, thanks. Now I'm **sad** / **happy**!

B **Look and write.**

1.

How are you today?

I'm _____tired_____ .

4.

What's the matter?

I'm _____ .

2.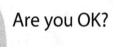

Are you OK?

Yes. I'm _____ , thanks.

5.

How _____ ?

I'm sad.

3.

What's _____ ?

Nothing's the matter!

6.

Are _____ ?

Yes. I'm fine, thanks.

A **Remember the video.** Circle the robots from the video.

1.

2.

3.

4.

B **Read and write.**

ASIMO the Robot

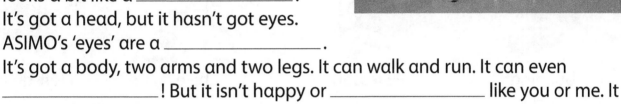

It's the school _____science_____ trip at the Miraikan Museum. Today, the students can see a real _____ called ASIMO. ASIMO is a 'humanoid' robot – it looks a bit like a _____. It's got a head, but it hasn't got eyes. ASIMO's 'eyes' are a _____. It's got a body, two arms and two legs. It can walk and run. It can even _____! But it isn't happy or _____ like you or me. It hasn't got feelings.

camera

happy

jump

man

robot

run

sad

science

A **Find and circle.** Then write.

r	m	u	c	o	o	l	s
s	m	a	t	h	s	p	h
w	h	i	k	d	n	e	w
h	o	m	e	w	o	r	k
e	g	b	o	a	t	n	n
r	e	a	d	i	n	g	y

1. c <u>o</u> <u>o</u> <u>l</u>

2. m __ __ __ __

3. n __ __

4. h __ __ __ __ __ __ __

5. b __ __ __

6. r __ __ __ __ __ __ __

B **Circle the odd one out.**

1.

building bricks

2.

PE lesson

3.

bike

4.

felt-tip pens

camera

art lesson

guitar

music lesson

tablet

robot

skateboard

tablet

C Read and write in the table.

~~bath~~   birthday   brother   thank   that   those

Words with *th* as in *maths*	Words with *th* as in *this*
bath	

D Look, read and circle.

1.

This is a felt-tip pen. / These are felt-tip pens.

2.

I've got music on Tuesday. / I've got music on Thursday.

3.

This is Amita's skateboard. / This isn't Amita's skateboard.

E Read and write.

1. Have you got science on Monday?   Yes, <u>I have</u>.

2. Are those your felt-tip pens?   No, _____.

3. Has she got science on Monday?   No, _____.

4. Has he got science on Monday?   Yes, _____.

5. Is this Milo's homework?   No, _____.

3 At Home

A **Listen and circle.** 🎧 TR: 3.1

door	mirror	bookcase	rug	floor

balcony	window	(armchair)	dining	room

B **Label the dining room.**

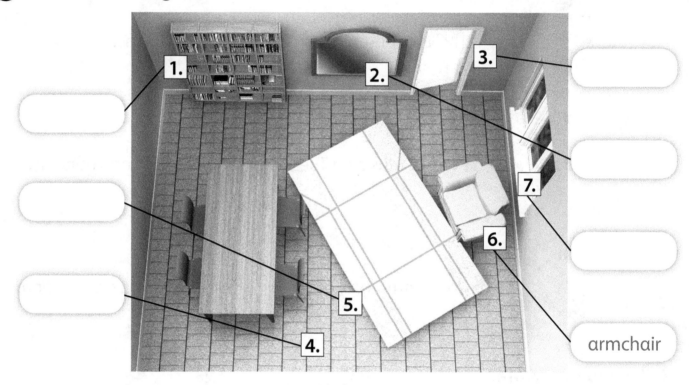

armchair

C **Colour the door, rug and armchair in Activity B.** Write about them.

In my picture:

1. There's a _____ door.

2. There's a _____ .

3. There's a _____ .

22

A **Listen and write.** 🎧 TR: 3.2

This is our home. This is _____ dining room.
That's their home. That's _____ dining room.

We've _____ a blue door and a rug on the floor.
They've _____ a blue door and a rug on the floor.

_____ a balcony with lots to see.
_____ a balcony with lots to see.

B **Read and circle.**

This is Paolo and Maria. This is (their)/ **your** tree house. They've **have** / **got** a rug on the floor. **We've** / **They've** got a bookcase with books and toys. They **'ve got** / **'s got** a guitar too. **Their** / **Our** tree house is cool!

A Circle the words that are opposites.

inside   stairs   wall   outside

B Read and write. TR: 3.3

climb   inside   outside   stairs   swing   wall

This is a plan for a small house in Denmark. Imagine we're in front of the door. Let's go _____!

There's a white armchair under the kitchen. Let's go up the _____.
There's a swing. A bookcase is behind the swing. I can sit on the _____ and read. How fun!

There's a bedroom and a small room with a computer. The bathroom is between these rooms.

Look! There's a climbing _____. We haven't got that in our house. Let's _____! I can see a garden with flowers. There's a balcony _____ too. This house is super cool!

C Read and write a tick (✓) or a cross (✗).

1. There's a bookcase.

2. There are two bathrooms.

3. There isn't a garden.

4. There isn't a dining room.

A Read and match.

1. The book is in front of the lamp.

2. The book is between the apple and the pencils.

3. The book is behind the computer.

B Listen and circle the things you hear. 🎧 TR: 3.4

C Look at the bedroom and write.

ball ~~bat~~ between bookcase door in front of

1. There's a _____bat_____ _____ the desk and the bed.

2. There's a _____ behind the _____.

3. There's a guitar _____ the _____.

A Listen and join the words. TR: 3.5

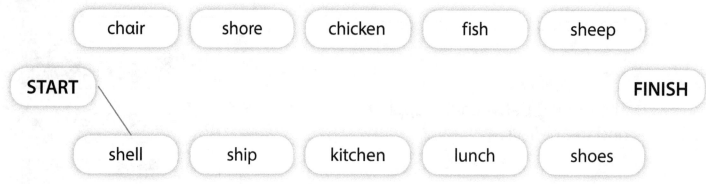

| chair | shore | chicken | fish | sheep |

START **FINISH**

| shell | ship | kitchen | lunch | shoes |

B Colour the words with *ch* yellow and the words with *sh* blue. Then say.

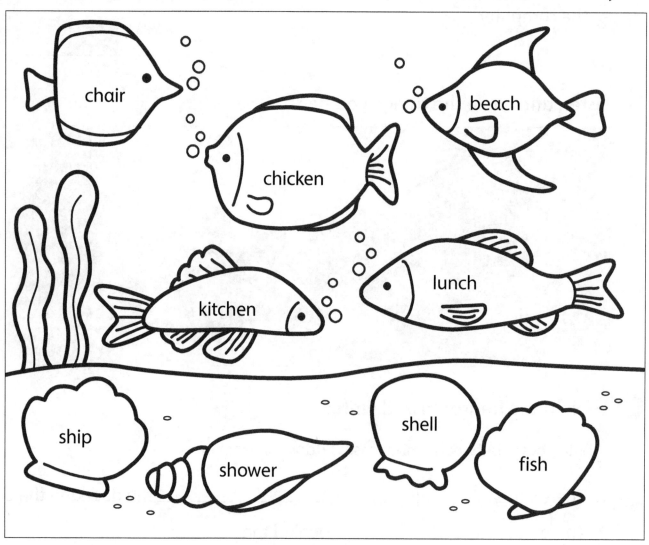

chair

chicken

beach

lunch

kitchen

ship

shower

shell

fish

Be kind to animals.

A Look and tick (✓).

☐ There's a spider on the balcony! You can look at it. But don't touch it.

☐ There's a spider on the balcony! Bring it inside and put it in a jar.

☐ There's a mouse in the kitchen! Catch it and put it in a jar.

☐ There's a mouse in the kitchen! Catch it and put it in the garden.

B Draw a picture of you being kind to animals.

4 Let's Play!

A **Find the words.** Circle.

1. 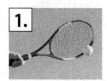	a	l	b	o	u	n	c	e	4. 
	c	a	t	c	h	s	d	g	
2. 	i	m	h	i	t	o	j	a	5. 
	d	k	j	u	m	p	p	a	
3. 	e	r	v	k	i	c	k	i	6. 
	s	r	g	t	h	r	o	w	

B **Listen and number.** Then write. 🎧 TR: 4.1

☐ 	☐ 	☐ 	1 
_____	_____	_____	_____

C **What do you do in each sport?** Write.

bounce   catch   hit   jump   kick   throw

football	hockey	basketball	tennis	baseball
jump kick throw				

28

A **Listen and write.** 🎧 TR: 4.2

We _____ baseball in the park,

and it's fun, fun, fun!

_____ throw, hit and catch the ball.

Then _____, run, run!

_____ run, jump and catch the ball.

Then _____, throw, throw!

We _____ or bounce the ball

in baseball. No, no, no!

B **Put the words in order.** Then match.

1. I / friends / hockey / play / with / my

<u>I play hockey with my friends</u> . | d |

2. kick / don't / the / you / ball / in / baseball

_____ . | |

3. tennis / play / they / outside

_____ . | |

4. we / basketball / run / the / with / ball / don't / in

_____ . | |

a.

b.

c.

d.

A Circle the word that means *great*. Underline the word that is a *group of people*.

different easy fantastic team

B Read and write. 🎧 TR: 4.3

basket different easy fantastic team

Do you like basketball? Lots of people do. In basketball, you run and bounce the ball.
You throw it to a player on your _____. You catch the ball, then you throw it in the _____ and ... score!

The King Charles Troupe is a group of basketball players from New York, US. Their game is _____.
They play on unicycles! A unicycle is like a bike but with one wheel, not two. It isn't _____.
The King Charles Troupe can bounce, throw and catch a ball – all on their unicycles.
They're _____! Lots of people watch them play.

C Answer the questions.

1. Do basketball players bounce the ball? _____.

2. Do players in the King Charles Troupe run with the ball? _____.

3. Has a unicycle got two wheels? _____.

4. Do you play a team sport? _____.

5. What sport is easy for you? _____.

A Read and circle.

1. Do you play baseball inside?   No, we **do** / **don't**.

2. Do basketball players throw the   Yes, they **do** / **don't**.
   ball into the basket?

3. Do you hit the ball in tennis?   **Yes** / **No**, you do.

4. Do you ride your bikes outside?   Yes, we **do** / **don't**.

5. Do they score goals in football?   **Yes** / **No**, they do.

B Listen and write. 🎧 TR: 4.4

1. Yes, I do _____.

2. _____.

3. _____.

4. _____.

C Write about you.

1.    Do you play _____? _____.

2.    Do you _____? _____.

A **Listen and number.** 🎧 TR: 4.5

pink ☐   sock ☐   black ☐

blank ☐   pick ☐   sink ☐

B **Make words with *ck* and *nk* to climb the rock.** Then say.

du   dri   ki   li   pi   ro   tha

duck

Be active.

A Look and tick (✓).

It's Saturday.

1. ☐ OK. Good idea.

2. ☐ No, let's go outside and play.

It's after school.

1. ☐ No, let's ride our bikes.

2. ☐ Yeah, OK.

B Read and draw.

Look at me! I'm active.

A Do the crossword.

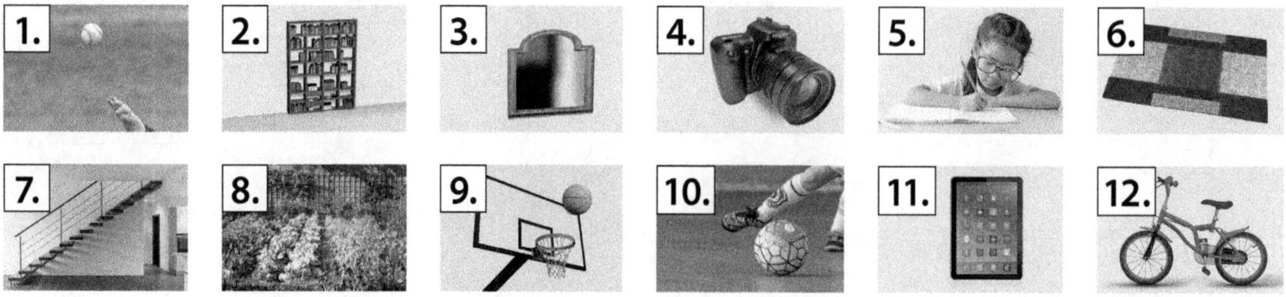

1. t
h
r
o
w

Let's Go on an Insect Safari!

A **Listen.** Tick (✓) the ones you hear. ⌒ TR: 4.6

lanternfly

bee

dragonfly

spider

B **Complete the table.** Listen again to check your answers. ⌒ TR: 4.7

	lanternfly	dragonfly	spider
How many legs has it got?			
What can it do?			

C **Imagine you're on an insect safari.** What do you find? Draw and write.

This is a _____.

It's _____.

It's got _____.

It can _____.

A **Unscramble the words.**

1.

m i r r o r

o m r i r r

2.

_ _ _ _ _ _

w o w d i n

3.

_ _ _

g r u

4.

_ _ _ _ _ _ _

o u n c e b

5.

_ _ _ _

m u p j

6.

_ _ _

t h i

B **Match.**

1. You walk up and down these.   fantastic

2. It's the opposite of *inside*.   rug

3. It's the opposite of *catch*.   dining room

4. It's on the floor.   stairs

5. You can eat dinner here.   throw

6. It means *great*.   outside

C Circle the odd one out: *ch, sh, ck, nk.*

1. chair   chicken   (sink)

2. think   ship   shower

3. sock   pink   sink

4. thank   think   fish

5. kitchen   shell   sheep

D Listen, draw and write. TR: 4.8

1.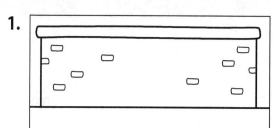

The tree is _____ the wall. The basketball is _____ the tree.

2.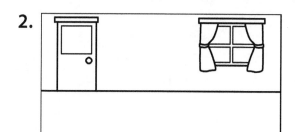

The mirror is _____ the door and the window. The rug is _____ the floor.

E Read and answer.

1. Do you play hockey at your school?

   _____.

2. Have you got a balcony outside your house?

   _____.

3. Have you got stairs inside your house?

   _____.

4. Do you play basketball outside your house?

   _____.

Lesson 1 Vocabulary

A Match.

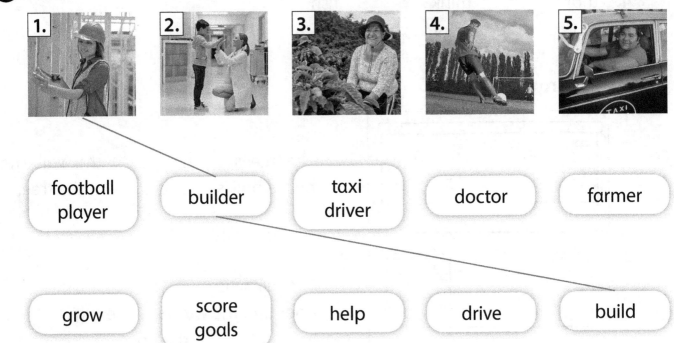

1. 2. 3. 4. 5.

football player   builder   taxi driver   doctor   farmer

grow   score goals   help   drive   build

B Listen and circle. 🎧 TR: 5.1

1. builder   doctor

2. teacher   doctor

3. taxi driver   farmer

4. football player   basketball player

C Write.

1. My _____aunt_____ is a _____taxi driver_____.

2. My _____ is a _____.

3. My _____ is a _____.

4. My _____ is a _____.

A Listen and write. TR: 5.2

This is a farmer. His name is Zaid.
He doesn't _____ apples.
He _____ olives instead!

This is a football player. Her name is Marisol.
She _____ hit the ball.
She _____ and _____ a goal!

B Look and write.

1. This teacher _____ maths.

2. She _____ English.

3. This man _____ tennis.

4. He _____ football.

A **Unscramble the words.**

1. krow _____

2. sue _____

3. boj _____

4. vrofaul _____

B **Read and write.** 🎧 TR: 5.3

flavour   job   twenty   use   work

Many people enjoy eating ice cream. Some people have got a favourite _____. There are lots of flavours! But do you know, you can work with ice cream? There's a job called an ice cream taster. It's fun, but ice cream tasters _____ hard too. To check each ice cream flavour, tasters _____ their eyes, nose and mouth. Does the ice cream look nice? Does it smell good? Does it taste good?

John Harrison is an ice cream taster. His day begins at 7:30 in the morning. He tastes ice cream for four to five hours. He tastes about _____ flavours three times each. Does he like his _____? Yes, he does!

C **Read and score from 1 (I don't agree) to 5 (I agree).**

1. Being an ice cream taster is easy.   1   2   3   4   5

2. Ice cream is my favourite food.   1   2   3   4   5

3. An ice cream taster is a cool job!   1   2   3   4   5

A Draw lines to make sentences.

1. Does — your brother — play football for the school?
   they

   Yes, he does.
        they do.

2. Does they like baseball too?
        he

   No, he don't.
        they doesn't.

B Listen and number. 🎧 TR: 5.4

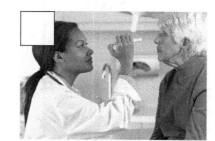

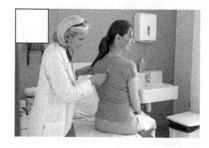

C Write about someone in your family.

1. Does your _____ work inside?   _____ .

2. Does _____ use a computer?   _____ .

3. Does _____ help people?   _____ .

4. Does _____ drive?   _____ .

5. Does _____ work with other people?   _____ .

A Listen and join the words. 🎧 TR: 5.5

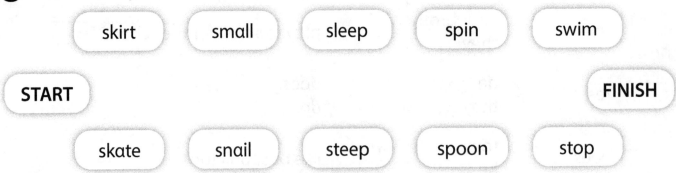

skirt small sleep spin swim

START FINISH

skate snail steep spoon stop

B Help the snail find the water. Find the words with *sk, sl, sm, sn, sp, st* or *sw*. Then say.

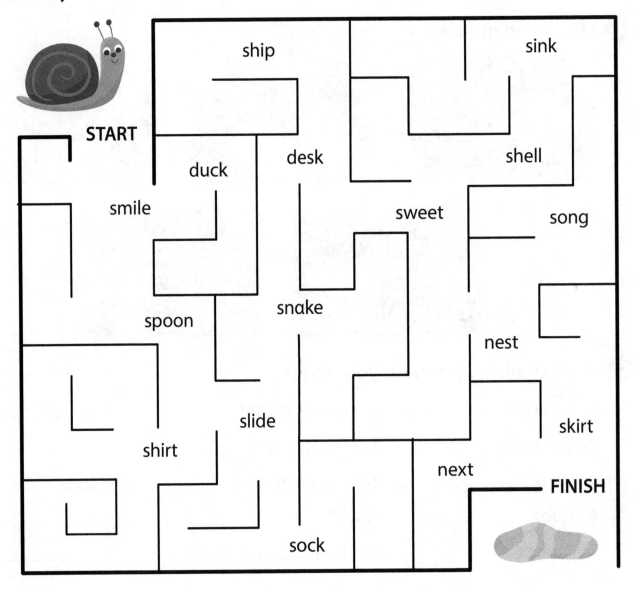

A Read and circle the polite phrases.

Thank you.   OK.   No.   Yes, please.

Come here.   Help me now!   No thanks.   Sorry, no.

B Look and tick (✓).

1.

a. Pass the rubber. ☐

b. Pass the rubber, please. ☐

2.

Would you like an apple?

a. No thanks, Dad. ☐

b. No, I don't. ☐

3.

Here we are.

a. Stop here. ☐

b. That's great, thank you. ☐

6 My Day

A **Listen and number.** 🎧 TR: 6.1

   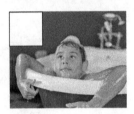

B **Look and write.**

> do   get   go   have

1. _____ up
2. _____ dressed
3. _____ breakfast
4. _____ lunch

5. _____ dinner
6. _____ homework
7. _____ a bath
8. _____ to bed

I do these things in this order: _____

C **What do you do in these rooms?**

1. I _____ in the kitchen.
2. I _____ in the living room.
3. I _____ in the bedroom.
4. I _____ in the bathroom.

A **Listen and write.** TR: 6.2

One o'clock, _____ o'clock, three o'clock, four.
Five o'clock, six _____, seven o'clock, more!

What's the _____ ? Tick-tock. It's seven o'clock.
Get up, _____ dressed. It's time for school!

What's the time? Tick-tock. It's _____ .
Have dinner, have a bath. _____ for bed!

B **Look and write the time.**

1.

It's four o'clock in the afternoon
_____ .

2.

_____
_____ .

3.

_____
_____ .

4.

_____
_____ .

A Find and circle three words from the reading.

c a h u r t e h w a i t u g f i n d o j

B Read and write. 🎧 TR: 6.3

finds   helps   hurt   waits

This is a story about the Blooms and a bird.

Mum gets _____. She can't walk.
One day, one of the boys _____ a
baby magpie. It's hurt too. The boy brings it
home. This bird is black and white, so they
call her 'Penguin'. The Blooms help Penguin
get better. Soon, she can fly!

Penguin _____ the Blooms too.
She sits with Mum in the afternoon. At three o'clock, Penguin goes to the
garden and _____. The boys come home from school. Now they can
play. With Penguin, the Blooms are happy again.

One day, Penguin flies away. Now she's with other birds!

C Put the sentences in order.

They call the bird Penguin. ☐

The bird is hurt. ☐

Mum gets hurt. 1

One boy finds a bird. ☐

Penguin flies away. ☐

Penguin helps the family. ☐

A **Put the words in the correct order.**

1. you / time / what / get / up / do / ?

   _____

2. get / up / we / six / o'clock / at / .

   _____

3. your / dad / time / does / what / bed / go / to / ?

   _____

4. he / o'clock / eleven / at / bed / goes / to / .

   _____

B **Listen and write the time in the clocks.** 🎧 TR: 6.4

1.

2.

3.

4.

C **Write what time you do each activity.**

1. get up: _I get up at_ _____.

2. have breakfast: _____.

3. get home: _____.

4. go to bed: _____.

A Listen and join the words. TR: 6.5

| black | class | gloves | plum | flag |

START   **FINISH**

| clock | glass | floor | glue | plane |

B Colour the picture. Then say.

bl = yellow
cl = orange
fl = green
gl = blue
pl = red

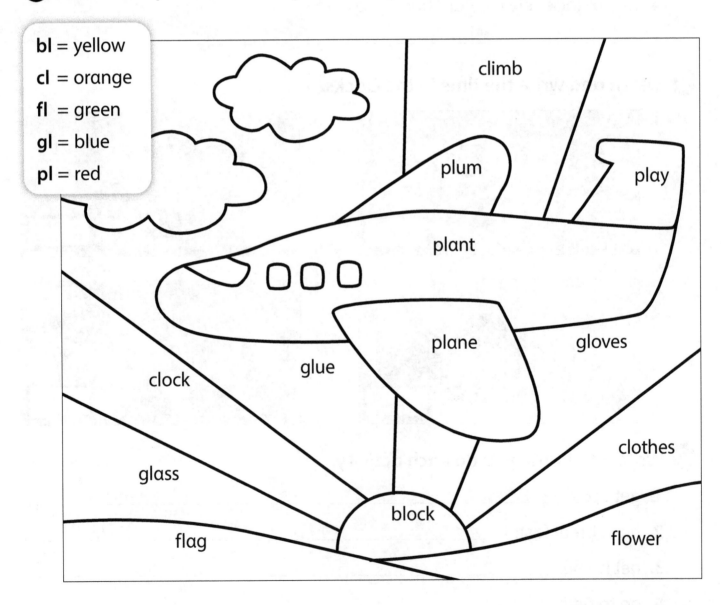

VALUE

Use your time well.

A **Who uses their time well?** Look and tick (✓).

1.

2.

3.

4.

B Read and draw.

This is me. Look! I use my time well.

A **Read and circle.** Then listen and check. 🎧 TR: 6.6

Karim: Hey, Ali! **Let's / Don't** play basketball.

Ali: OK, that **looks / sounds** like fun.

Karim: Imran, do you want to play basketball too?

Imran: **Not / No** really. I want to play football. Is that OK?

Ali: **Not. / No.** I don't want to play football.

Karim: Well, we can play basketball and football!

Imran: **Good / Bad** idea!

Ali: Come on. Let's go to the **library / park.**

B **Listen and tick (✓) *a* or *b*.** 🎧 TR: 6.7

	a	b
1. Let's go to the swimming pool.	✓	
2. Do you want to play hockey?		
3. We can play football and ride our bikes.		
4. I don't want to go for a walk.		
5. Come on. Let's have a snack.		
6. Do you want to watch TV at my house?		

A **Remember the video.** Circle the things astronauts have got.

1. 2. 3. 4.

B **Read and write T (true) or F (false).**

1. Earth looks green and blue from space.   F

2. There are lots of astronauts on the ISS.

3. Everything floats in outer space.

4. Sometimes the astronauts work outside the space station.

5. The astronauts don't live on the ISS. They go home to Earth in the evening.

6. The astronauts can do exercise on the ISS.

C **Imagine you're an astronaut on the ISS.** It's time to get up. Draw two things you do. (Remember that everything floats!)

1.

2.

Ⓐ Match.

1. do   dressed

2. score   a bath

3. drive   homework

4. have   English

5. go   houses

6. teach   goals

7. build   to bed

8. get   a taxi

Ⓑ Find and circle seven words.

x (u s e) p f l a v o u r h w o r k n h u r t p j o b r w a i t u f i n d q

Ⓒ Look and write.

1.

 __ __ oon

2.

 __ __ ag

3.

 __ __ um

4.

 __ __ ock

5.

 de __ __

6.

 ne __ __

D **Read and circle.**

This is Clarita. She's a taxi driver. She **gets up** / **get up** at seven o'clock **at** / **in** the morning. She doesn't **works** / **work** in the morning. She goes to work at one o'clock in the afternoon. She **drives** / **drive** her taxi around town. She doesn't **has** / **have** dinner at home. She **goes** / **go** to bed at twelve o'clock.

E **Read and answer.**

1. What time does Clarita get up?

   _____.

2. What time do you get up?

   _____.

3. Does Clarita go to work in the afternoon?

   _____.

4. What time do you go to school?

   _____.

5. Does Clarita go to bed at one o'clock in the morning?

   _____.

6. What time do you go to bed?

   _____.

7 Mealtime

A Match.

1. juice
2. egg
3. beans
4. sausage
5. cheese
6. pear
7. chips
8. grapes
9. mango
10. chicken

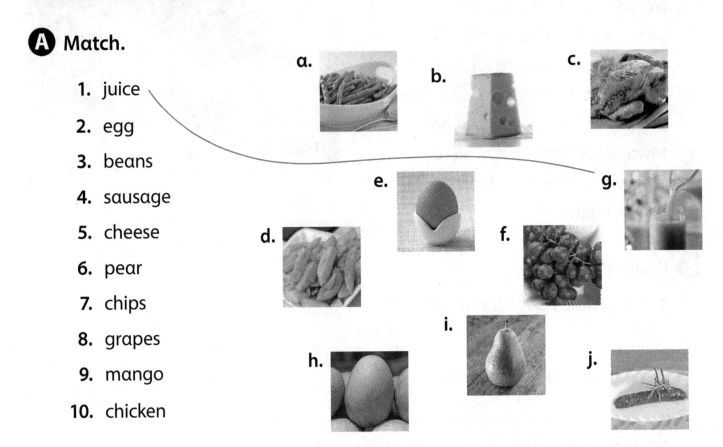

B Listen and circle the food or drink each person likes. TR: 7.1

1. mango juice / pear juice
2. chips / beans
3. cheese / eggs
4. sausage / chicken

C What do you like? Write six foods in order from ☹ to ☺.

☹ _____   _____   _____

_____   _____   _____

A Listen and write. TR: 7.2

What have we got for breakfast today?
There's _____ bread, an egg, some orange juice too.
But _____ isn't any milk!
Oh, what can we do?

What have we got for lunch today?
_____ rice, some grapes, a mango too.
But _____ any chicken!
Oh, what can we do?

What have we got for dinner today?
_____ chips, some beans, some carrots too.
But _____ sausages!
Oh, what can we do?

B Read and circle.

This is my breakfast. **There / There's**
an egg. There's **a / some** bread
and **there's / there are** some
sausages. There **is / isn't** any juice,
but there's some milk. There aren't
any / some oranges, but there's
some / a pear. It's a big breakfast.

A Circle the food.

burger   get   money   put

B Read and write. 🎧 TR: 7.3

> burger get money pizza put snack

You're feeling hungry and you want a _____. You can find one in a vending machine. Just _____ your _____ in, and there it is! People usually buy sweets and drinks from vending machines, but you can get much more.

Some vending machines have got bread and eggs. Do you eat fruit? You can _____ oranges or bananas too.

Is there any food for lunch and dinner in a vending machine? Yes, there is! You can get a _____, or you can get chicken and rice. A vending machine can even make a _____ for you!

Vending machines have got other things too: socks, jeans, books ... even cars!

C Circle the things you can't find in a vending machine.

a car   a house   a burger   a tree   a pizza   an egg

A Read and write.

a   any   are   aren't   is   isn't

1. Is there _____ milk?   Yes, there _____.

2. Is there _____ mango?   No, there _____.

3. _____ there any beans?   No, there _____.

B Listen and write *Diego* or *Luis*. 🎧 TR: 7.4

1. _____   2. _____

C Look at the pictures in Activity B. Write.

Diego's Lunch

1. juice   _____Is there any juice_____?   _____Yes, there is_____.

2. pear   _____?   _____.

3. carrots   _____?   _____.

Luis's Lunch

4. mango   _____?   _____.

5. burger   _____?   _____.

6. beans   _____?   _____.

A **Listen and circle.** 🎧 TR: 7.5

frog   present   great   green   draw   crab   breakfast

tree   crayon   drink   train   friend   pretty   brother

B **Where is the treasure?** Follow the path. Complete the words. Then say.

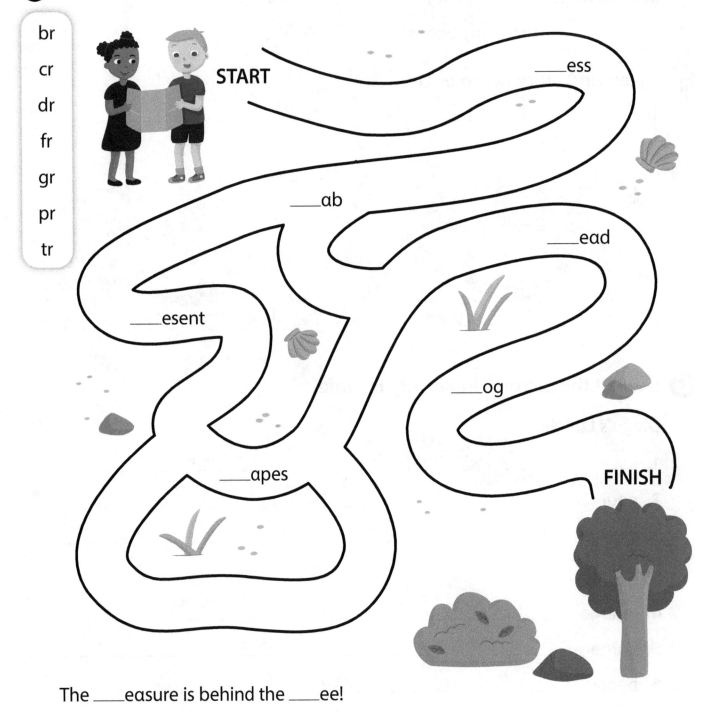

br

cr

dr

fr

gr

pr

tr

START

____ess

____ab

____ead

____esent

____og

____apes

FINISH

The ____easure is behind the ____ee!

VALUE
Give and share.

A Look and tick (✓).

1.

2.

3.

B Read and draw.

Look at me! I can give and share.

8 Celebrate!

A **Listen and join.** 🎧 TR: 8.1

a.

d.

1. hold   with my friends

2. take   lemonade   b.   e.

3. listen   ice cream

4. dance   a balloon

5. eat   to music   c.   f.

6. drink   photos

B **Read and write.**

> dance   drink   eat   hold   music   photos

1. Can you _____ this present for me, please?

2. Can I _____ this juice, please?

3. Can you take _____, please?

4. Can we _____ the cake now?

5. Let's _____!

6. Let's listen to _____!

C **How do you celebrate?** Draw and write.

1. I _____
_____.

2. We _____
_____.

3. _____
_____.

A **Listen and write.** TR: 8.2

It's my birthday. I'm eight today.
We're _____ a party – hurray, hurray!

_____ holding balloons and playing a game.
We're _____ cake and drinking lemonade.
My classmates are here and _____ fun.
_____ so happy. Thank you, everyone!

It's my birthday. I'm eight today.
_____ a party – hurray, hurray!

B **Look and write.**

1. She _____ photos.

2. He _____ an apple.

3. The boys _____.

4. The girls _____.

Ⓐ Unscramble the words. Which one can you hold? Tick (✓) the word.

1. valifest _____ ☐   **3.** teckub _____ ☐

2. joyen _____ ☐   **4.** tseret _____ ☐

Ⓑ Read and write. 🎧 TR: 8.3

> bucket   enjoying   festival   parties   street   water

It's the Songkran _____ in
Thailand, and people – young and old –
are having fun. This is the New Year for
Thai people. The festival usually goes
on for three days. There are lots of street
_____. People go outside and
have big _____ fights. At this
festival, you can throw water on your friends,
your family ... everyone. It's fantastic!

Look at this family. They're _____ Songkran. They've got buckets of
water. This boy is holding a _____ of water. What is he doing with
that water? He's throwing it on the people in the _____! Is that OK?
Yes, of course! It's Songkran!

Ⓒ Answer the questions about Songkran and a festival that you enjoy.

	Songkran	**My festival**
1. How many days does it go on for?		
2. What do you do at the festival?		
3. Why do you celebrate it?		

A Put the words in the correct order.

1. you / are / what / doing / ?

   _____

   taking / I'm / photos / .

   _____

2. your / doing / what's / brother / ?

   _____

   guitar / he's / his / playing / .

   _____

3. they / what / doing / are / ?

   _____

   fight / having / they're / water / a / .

   _____

B Listen and tick (✓). 🎧 TR: 8.4

1. ☐ ☐

3. ☐ ☐

2. ☐ ☐

4. ☐ ☐

C Write.

1. What are you doing?

   I'm _____.

2. _____?

   My classmates are playing computer games.

A **Listen and join the words.** 🎧 TR: 8.5

| thing | sink | bang | long | rink |

START

FINISH

| think | sing | bank | link | ring |

B **Help the sheep cross the bridge.** Write words with *ng* or *nk* to build the bridge. Then say.

dri   lo   morni   pi   si   so   stri   ta   thi

drink

VALUE

Be grateful.

A Look and tick (✓).

1.

2.

B Circle all the things that you are grateful for.

I've got some cool toys.

I've got good friends.

My grandparents
live near my house.

My family helps me with
my English homework.

Be grateful!

I've got a bike.

I've got a pet.

I've got homework today.

I've got some books.

C Read, write and draw.

This is something I'm grateful for:

_____

_____

_____

_____

A Find and circle.

go to bed · eggs · juice · builder · taxi driver · balloon · bucket

take a photo · do homework · burger · have dinner · football player

Pizza Village: A Pizza Festival in Naples

A **Listen.** Tick (✓) the pizza toppings you hear. 🎧 TR: 8.6

☐ eggs ☐ cheese

☐ tomato ☐ juice

☐ vegetables ☐ meat

B **Underline the incorrect information.** Then correct it.

1. The festival is in <u>Milan</u>, Italy. _____Naples_____

2. The favourite pizza at the festival has got tomato and egg on it. _____

3. At the festival, people can watch TV, dance and take photos. _____

4. People can't learn how to make pizza at the festival. _____

C **Imagine you are at a food festival.** Complete the table.

1. When is the festival?	
2. How many days is the festival?	
3. What activities can people do at the festival?	

A Circle the odd one out.

1.
hold   dance   beans

3.
mango   balloon   pear

2.
chicken   lemonade   juice

4.
listen to   take   sausage
music   photos

B Find and circle. Then write.

r	m	o	n	e	y	f	w
e	a	t	t	b	v	s	a
o	c	h	e	e	s	e	k
f	e	s	t	i	v	a	l
i	r	n	d	r	i	n	k
u	t	e	n	j	o	y	z

1. m __ __ __y

2. e __ __

3. ch __ __ __ __

4. f __ __ __ __v __l

5. dr __ __ __

6. e __ __ __y

C Read and write.

br cr dr fr gr ng pr tr

1. I've got some __ __apes for lunch.

2. There's some __ __ead in the bag.

3. This is a __ __esent for you!

4. This __ __ee is very big.

5. Look! There's a green __ __og.

6. Look! There's a big __ __ab.

7. We can si__ __ at the party.

8. That is my __ __ess.

D Read and circle.

1. I'm **hold** / **holding** a present.
2. There's **a** / **some** cheese.
3. There **are** / **is** some pears.
4. **We're** / **We** listening to music.
5. What are you **do** / **doing**?
6. Is there **a** / **any** juice?

E Look and write.

1. Are there any balloons at the party?

   _____ .

2. What's the mum doing?

   _____ .

3. Are there any burgers on the table?

   _____ .

4. (What / grandpa)

   _____ ?

   He's eating cake.

5. (What / children)

   _____ ?

   They're dancing.

Word List

Welcome	Unit 1	Unit 2	Unit 3	Unit 4
eleven	art	bike	armchair	baseball
twelve	bath	brother	balcony	basketball
thirteen	birthday	building bricks	bookcase	bounce
fourteen	boat	camera	chair	catch
fifteen	computers	cool	dining room	different
sixteen	English	felt-tip pens	door	duck
seventeen	homework	guitar	fish	easy
eighteen	lesson	new	floor	fantastic
nineteen	maths	old	inside	hit
twenty	music	robot	lunch	hockey
black	PE	skateboard	mirror	jump
blue	reading	tablet	outside	kick
brown	river	these	rug	pink
green	science	this	ship	sink
orange	Thursday		stairs	socks
purple			wall	team
red			window	tennis
white				throw
yellow				
arm				
ear				
eye				
foot				
hand				
head				
leg				
mouth				

Unit 5	Unit 6	Unit 7	Unit 8
build	black	beans	angry
builder	clock	bread	balloon
doctor	do homework	burger	bucket
drive	have a bath	cheese	dance
farmer	have breakfast	chicken	drink
flavour	have dinner	chips	eat
football player	have lunch	crab	enjoy
grow	find	dress	festival
help	flag	egg	hold
job	get dressed	frog	lemonade
score goals	get up	get	listen to music
skirt	glass	grapes	long
slide	go to bed	juice	ring
small	hurt	mango	sing
snack	plum	money	take photos
spoon	wait	pear	
stop		present	
swim		put	
taxi driver		sausage	
use		tree	
work			